CHANGE AS A
CURVED EQUATION

ALSO BY DONALD EVERETT AXINN

POETRY

Sliding down the Wind
The Hawk's Dream and Other Poems
Against Gravity
The Colors of Infinity
Dawn Patrol
The Latest Illusion

FICTION

Spin
The Ego Makers

CHANGE AS A CURVED EQUATION

Poems

DONALD EVERETT AXINN

INTRODUCTION BY JAY PARINI

ARCADE PUBLISHING • NEW YORK

FIRST EDITION

ISBN 1-55970-636-8
Library of Congress Control Number 2002109943
Library of Congress Cataloging-in-Publication Information is
available.

Published in the United States by Arcade Publishing, Inc., New York
Distributed by AOL Time Warner Book Group

Visit our Web site at www.arcadepub.com

10   9   8   7   6   5   4   3   2   1

Designed by API

CCP

PRINTED IN THE UNITED STATES OF AMERICA

The most beautiful experience we can have is the mysterious
. . . the fundamental emotion which stands at the cradle of
true art and true science.

—Albert Einstein

To make an apple pie from scratch you must first start with
the universe.

—Carl Sagan

The poet holds up a piece of the world. We see it glowing
with a strange, emotional fire.

—Christopher Caldwell

CONTENTS

Author's Note   *xi*

Acknowledgments   *xiii*

Introduction by Jay Parini   *xv*

I   Reality and Change Are Linked Like Lovers

Change as a Curved Equation   3

Washed in the Flame of a Small Galaxy   6

Over the Ardennes, 2000   7

Equality   8

Sky   9

Examination   10

Ancient Messages   11

Reverie   12

Nightmare   13

Decisions   14

Night Songs   15

Power   16

Where Light and Time Began   17

Echoes in the Morning Sun   18

II   I Don't Know What to Do About the Daffodil

First Love   21

Shadow   23

promise   24

Until He Asked Me   25

Quetzalcoatl and Leonardo   26

Yes, This Rain, This Summer Rain   27

III   Floating on Air Fat with Clarity and Purpose

Signals   31

Yaqui Universe   32

Denali   33

Something in the Forest   34

Makah Country   35

Middlebury July   37

Saudi Arabia   39

Sitka   41

On the Alpine Highlands   42

Taos Revisited   43

The Loner   44

Scene   46

The Longhouse   47

IV   The Way Forward, The Way Back

Mathematics for a Rainy Morning   51

Winter's Eloquence   52

On a Clear Winter Night   53

Four for Winter   54

Music of the Meadow   55

January Twilight   56

Great White Pine   57

The Fog   58

Stearman   59

At Five Hundred Feet, New York to Florida   61

Wings   62

Winter Storm   63

Winterscape   64

The Way Forward, The Way Back   65

About the Author   67

AUTHOR'S NOTE

We are part of an extraordinary and complex design. The artist can make life livable and bring harmony. It has been said that art is "a mirror in which we catch glimpses of ourselves." It may not make us successful or powerful, but art can bring a measure of meaning to existence.

ACKNOWLEDGMENTS

I wish to thank Dick and Jeannette Seaver for their continued faith in my writing, and to Beverly Carr, my superb assistant.

And Joan for her support and sparkle.

Finally, a tribute to my fellow poets, who recognize the world for what it is and choose to create light in which to better see existence.

INTRODUCTION

Robert Pinsky eloquently said of the initial poem in this new collection, *Change as a Curved Equation*, "Don Axinn's title poem thinks in language the way Donne and Marvell did, so that the geometry of curves and lines, heights and perspectives, comes alive: phrases like 'it comes down to' and 'gravity' take on the extra vibrations known as poetry." Gravity, it seems, has deep metaphorical value for Axinn, who has always struck me as a poet of flight.

His work, in poetry and prose, considers the symbolic trajectory of human experience, the journey into regions of mystery and exhilaration, and the sense of loss (with gains of wisdom) that accompanies the fall to earth. In this latest volume, he examines—in the title poem and throughout the collection—the way memories and dreams "curve back to some beginning / we might better understand." In effect, this book represents an attempt to understand, more deeply, the mysterious point of origin that constitutes both a beginning and an end.

Anyone familiar with Axinn's work will recognize the markers that connect to his earlier poems. There is the same preoccupation with certain landscapes—especially the landscape of Vermont which he describes beautifully in various poems. Even here, in poems of place, his gaze turns naturally upward, as in "Sky," where he writes:

I revere the sky
That brought my children
The place where I fly,
And play on the fields of gods.

There is a reverence throughout his work for banks of clouds, the changes of light, the contours of the experience.

As ever, Axinn keeps watch on the natural world, as in "Winter's Eloquence," where he says: "Winter is impeccably white and elegant; / Its pronouncement offered today is / snow / cold sandy granules / Fashioned from a disheveled sky." That word *disheveled* here, for example, is unexpected, and it shocks the reader into a recognition of some aspect of experience that lay previously buried. Many of these poems about nature, as one might expect, turn toward elegy and celebration, as in "Yes, This Rain, This Summer Rain," a lovely poem in which he praises "our magnificent summer rain" with a sense of ecstasy.

The oscillation of the seasons, the journey through various stages of life, the motions of the mind through time and place: these are the preoccupations that readers will discover in these poems. Axinn has a keen eye for detail, and his observations are often memorable, as in "The Way Forward, The Way Back," which opens with a moment of visual scrutiny:

The leaf hesitates then pitches forward
From the ash tree onto my deck and acts confused
Not sure of its way down.

This image becomes, in the course of the poem, a metaphysical one, a point of speculation, from which the poet perambulates "into the universe on its mission to deliver the leaf."

Axinn is that rare breed of poet who knows what it's like to work in the so-called real world: he has built up a company of his own, has been a highly successful real estate developer and investor. He has traveled widely, as a man of business and a man of letters. These various experiences have shaped his work, as has his family life and his Jewish-American heritage. These elements all play into and through the poems in interesting and productive ways.

The poems are sometimes playful and teasing, sometimes heartfelt, sometimes meditative. These are poems of love, poems about flying, poems about children, and poems about nature. But the voice behind the poems remains consistent, and is recognizable as that of Donald Everett Axinn, a writer who has cultivated a special tone and sensibility over many years. *Change as a Curved Equation* represents an admirable addition to that sensibility, modifying and extending themes previously examined.

It was Robert Frost who famously suggested that a poem should "begin in delight and end in wisdom." Axinn seems to have taken Frost to heart in this regard. But he has not done so abstractly, as Robert Pinsky has suggested. His poems think in language, where all poems must—however airborne in principle—remain grounded.

—JAY PARINI

I

REALITY AND CHANGE ARE LINKED LIKE LOVERS

CHANGE AS A CURVED EQUATION

I

The universe
           perhaps
           curves back
           and around.
At twilight my antique WACO biplane
                     and I lift off
                     the grass airstrip
To rummage around the Champlain Valley
                     to be reassured by
                     Otter Creek the Green
                     and Adirondack Mountains.
We pursue familiar lines and circles
                     for answers
But sometimes it feels like
                     we could be flying
                     with existence in reverse.

II

Think of a ball:
           it cannot comprehend
           or tolerate
           the concept of corners.

III

Stephen Hawking
    suggests that the elements
    dance effortlessly in a cosmos
    of gravity and space and time
While we attempt to deal
        with events in a world
        down here (or up there if you prefer)
        that change and keep on changing.

IV

Reality and change
        are linked like lovers.
        If you pretend things won't ever change
        beware of explosions
A big bang
    in your face
    in your heart
    in every presumption
Except if you believe
        you possess a spirit
        that protects you forever.
But does this spirit
        teach you about the curves
        and corners
        that define your life?

V

Perhaps
    memories dreams and fantasies
    curve back to some beginning
    we might better understand.
It comes down
      to decoding
      the meaning of change
      if it curves
      or travels a straight line.

WASHED IN THE FLAME
OF A SMALL GALAXY

for Jenny

Jenny waits 3,000 moon-shaped miles away
In Berkeley as I streak to be with her
This daughter of mine
                whom time has washed
In the flame of a small galaxy
                where only certain children
Are born, those who can feel
                the brightest clouds
                and lead the rest of us
To the edges of our worlds
Up the mountains of our lives
Instructing us to part the curtains
                demand light
And share it with those who have trouble
                stepping out of the shadows.

This is Jennifer, from that small galaxy,
                who broke the code
                right from the beginning.

OVER THE ARDENNES, 2000

Eighty-five years later we speed high
Over the forest where soft-faced boys,
Unsuspecting actors in a diabolical comedy,
Saviors of their countries, like Arthur
And his knights, jousted in their
Small wood and linen-covered biplanes,
Flying over a countryside parading haze,
Where sky and land melded at their borders.
These naïve warriors maneuvered to shoot
Each other out of noise-splattered air,
Burning airplanes cutting holes that
Still exist but cannot be readily seen.

But now time brings us together and we watch
Them twist and turn, toy miniatures there
Below us in a living diorama of death,
The time of then merging with the now.

Look, one tails the other,
His bullets climb the fuselage
To reach the silk-scarved pilot,
His glory suddenly shot into eternity.
He waves to his adversary,
Slumps forward and spins into French soil.
Perhaps the victor was my grandfather.

EQUALITY

This sun-sponsored morning
Sweeps through tasseled grasses
     and spread-armed trees
Into expectant nooks and corners
     of a hawk-eyed landscape
Not concerned about which of us
Is burdened from memories
We've carried through our nation's scalded history
Where you were star-crossed
           if you came out
Black or red or yellow
           if your god
Was not like theirs.
Observe children, their small sounds
Splashing laughing.
           And listen to the dead.
           We may still be able to boost
     our frayed limbs into the sky
On fickle winds that spread
Passions along dark folds
           of clouds
Designed to expose the ashes
           along with the truth.

SKY

I revere the sky
that brought my children
the place where I fly
and play on the fields of gods.

Oh, but there is more:
to ride on air that offers
a life and death devoid
of gravity's suppressions,

and liberation
        from trumpery,
        from tales told by idiots,
        from the weight of experience,

        from the hurt of knowledge,
        from the pain
        for those loved,

        whom I will join
        in that next place from which
        I cannot talk to you.

EXAMINATION

In these later years,
            at 4 A.M. or 4 P.M.
I try to understand who and what I have become.

I look at sunrises and sunsets,
            never see the exact same composition
            and combination of colors.
I observe my face in mirrors,
Seeking more than I already know.
            I listen more carefully,
            especially when I talk to myself.

I read this. I understand more.
            But doubts and confusion
            remain.
About our behavior and how what we say to each other
            too often ends up with the wrong consequence.
Why light and gravity and truth sometimes seem
            such unsolvable mysteries.
How mathematics is a comforting constant,
            but the true constant is change.
That energy cannot be created nor destroyed,
            but changes in strange ways.
And especially how time is not always timely
            but controls all my lives.

ANCIENT MESSAGES

Here   exploring a sky
                        full of mystery
                        and timeless time

Where   fat happy cumulus
                        are like cousins
                        dressed in ancestral shades
                        of whites, off-whites, and grays
                        at a family reunion

Where   cauliflowered clouds
                        shove bulbous tops
                        up against their limit,
                        finally restrained
                        by meticulous temperature
                        that pulls them apart

Where   virgas try but fail
                        to emancipate enriched
                        moisture that hangs
                        like wet sheets on a summer day

Here   there are pregnant winds
                        carrying other ancient messages
                        waiting for us to hear them.

REVERIE

Earthbound, then unbound to where angels love secrets,
        their whispers draped lightly over clouds
            stuffed with questions.
Up here time loses its past but also its future.
Below the world is spread thick with the colors
        of everything, of nothing.
Nothing is new, everything is new. You must know
        the players and translate
           their languages.
I have trouble accepting the way things are.
Only those who do not know
           offer suggestions.
See this blanket made of dreams and fantasies?
        It's too heavy to pull over my eyes.
But that's all right. I can talk like this, speculate
        about fire and stars and gravity.
I like artists, but worry when they confront reality.
You keep telling me I'm crazy, but that's how I cope.
In any event, thanks, Charles. Charles Wright,
        for your poems and how they light the way.

NIGHTMARE

You are a vampire I cannot escape.
        I weaken with every suck
Succumbing to your wrath.

You are the fiend gone berserk
        a drunken foul-breathed dragon.
You raze my cities and scorch my savannas.
        Your flames sear my flesh.

You are the scaled terror clanging down the hall
        in my most heinous dream.
You are everything I have ever loathed.
        I must find a way
                to kill you.

DECISIONS

You! So much like Hamlet,
Fogged in the fear that shackles you

In the mists mesmerizing Elsinore.
Listen: the ghost of your father clangs,

Warning you to rip off
The chains of hesitation

You've cinched so tightly around you.
Fool! You may have one last chance

To reach the parapets and comprehend
Clearly all you would observe.

Damn you! Shove away indecision,
Watch it crash down below.

Time sprints away, shortening the lease
Created for your life; it becomes

Your exacting companion and swirls
Inside your head, its winds waiting

To strip your armor, blow it into eternity,
With you leading the way.

NIGHT SONGS

A chorus
>> of apparently deaf crickets
>> congregate
somewhere out of sight,
>> prattling incessantly
>> in their two-note
staccatos.

Their buddies,
>> the bullfrogs,
>> take over
the discourse
>> and begin to belch out
>> their bizarre love songs.

A night heron
>> and perhaps a loon
>> screech
complaining about the cacophony.

POWER

I sit here motionless.
   The april sun
   bakes winter out.
The sun instructs
   me about power.

WHERE LIGHT AND TIME BEGAN

We can only speculate when light began.
Picture this:
        X rays bolting out from the center
        of galaxies at a time before candescent
Beams of light, bright beyond imagining,
Began their lives waving across the universe.

A better question is when did time begin?

I once heard about a scientist who, close to death,
        tried to sum up his life.
"I never really understood it," he said,
        his eyes hollow staring toward infinity.
"The enigma, the miracle of simply being
                born, living, then dying."

ECHOES IN THE MORNING SUN

I want what you want:

An invitation from the morning sun,
Rays
That capture the speech of birds
That record the giggles of children
Who revel in new games
And make friends with their unfurling bodies.

Sleep is different.

Sleep offers echoes of parents, children, lovers,
Suppressed intimacies or terrors,
Lasting imprints with which we live.

We must give up control,

Probe the core
And essence of our lives,
Ferret out reflected memories,
Quintessential echoes beamed
Forward into the now,
Then forward again
So that we may migrate
Less blindly
                        into tomorrow.

II

I DON'T KNOW WHAT TO DO ABOUT THE DAFFODIL

FIRST LOVE

that day noisy in the phone
booth the trucks on the expressway
I called you I did every day
wanted to needed to feel
complete my stunted mind
crippled with immaturity
a bad excuse for my narcissism you knew that
you loved me anyway
what others had to confront
you did when they told you
it was leukemia
gift gift gift wonder
daffodils rich gold yellow the sun
those snappy expectant April mornings
when we can't conceive of anything
going wrong you took my hand once see
look at this one it unfolds like we do
remember I remember
every spring your expression flushed
you taught me sometimes we'd pull
off the road in the bushes
front seat back seat against the car
the rest of the world abandoned
sleep we shared afterward in bed so many beds
on the floor try to understand you said what's
happening it's all right no please I
begged you can't go how can I live I did

you didn't every spring I kneel next to one
particular daffodil I say your name today again
I don't know what to do about the daffodil

SHADOW

You scamper across my vision
Leaning forward for a kiss.
Imp! Mischief maker!
You grin, your fingers wend
Across my lips
Wisping slowly down my back.
You make my breath jagged.
I try to remember the first time
But passion always loses its memory.

PROMISE

march clouds gesture
race across the sky
replacing winter's
grayed canopy of sleep
                    soon
the colors of renewal
will wake check the scene
begin to flow then surge
picking familiar places
to shout "spring"
yet one more time

UNTIL HE ASKED ME

He flew airplanes as if he had to,
  embracing them like lovers,
coupled, merged, rising together
  from constrained earth, gulping air
like a whale bursting from the sea,
  immersed in the skies he adored.

  He was the father I knew on the ground
but never really above it,
  until he asked me before he died
to cremate the hell out of him, toss his ashes out,
  pretend he was taking his last breath,
  the one he would carry into eternity.

QUETZALCOATL AND LEONARDO

First, I was Quetzalcoatl the Aztec,
Blond God of the Air, plumed serpent,
Poet bird who carried the morning reds
And rainbowed sunsets to all my people.

Then, Leonardo da Vinci, descended
From the birds, obsessed with flight,
Dreaming of explorers who would spring off
The ground released from harbored constraints.

You can fly with me, my feathered arms
To carry us up on pink and pale blue winds.
We tumble over and over, folded
Into one on a wet bed of frisky clouds.

YES, THIS RAIN, THIS SUMMER RAIN

This fertile rain, dispensed like air
           gifted at birth,
is at last delivered onto the parched
               hot-blooded land.
               It responds the way you do
when you want me to touch you.

This erotic rain, its lust released, is guided
           by musk suffused in dispersed light
           by aroused semen-filled clouds
spread across where you lie and wait.

At first the rain teases, then roars,
           shouting and dominating;
           its energy bangs with fists
of lightning flung here then there, affirmed whacks
           and claps of its virility.

Slowly at first, then in remembered rhythms,
you stir, reach up, all of you primed,
           imploring me to plunge down
           and possess you. And then
as you inhale me, you become whetted
           in ways you had almost forgotten,
recollecting conjugated intimacies
           you believed had abandoned you.

Wake up. Yes, I am really here,

renewal implanted
in the smells we make,
in bewitched songs we compose.
I have indeed waited for you, as you have for me.

Yes, this rain, our magnificent summer rain.

III

FLOATING ON AIR
FAT WITH
CLARITY AND PURPOSE

SIGNALS

I

Kindling is lit, logs blaze,
Flames climb like fingers aroused,
               impulsive, passionate.
They illuminate the present and are packed
               with moss-backed memories
               that suggest the future.

II

Now envision a lighthouse beacon.
Look—it signals the truth!
               "Go here, do not go there."
We build our vessels out of logic and faith,
Sailors, hitchhikers riding on swells
               of anticipation,
Voyagers migrating on foam-crested time,
The imperative that mandates the tides
               of our lives.

III

We are destined to witness how pretentiousness
Burns out, even as we mutter false heroics,
               attempting to deny mortality.

YAQUI UNIVERSE

When you waited alone through the night
        lying on the terra-cotta bluff
        to dream of buffalo and deer
        you watched the dark winds
dispatch the stars into their sleep.

        When you witnessed the dawn arrive
            smoky gray, then change to crimson,
        powder blue, then change to azure,
you understood how the gods cause
        the light to spill down into the sky.

Then you became the universe.
Then, you became the universe.

DENALI

This speck, our diminutive seaplane,
Hangs boldly, seems out of place.
My eyes are riveted on the Alaskan Range,
On Denali, ensconced like a king
        holding court. His queen,
Foraker, sits in judgment next to him.
Both are sheered in clothes of granite,
Their whitened crevices bulky, weighed down
By cascading snows packed into glaciers
That move silently, imperceptibly,
        their lines of browned avalanche dirt
Captured slowly over the centuries.
I peer down on death but also on life
And have this feeling
        I am also looking out on God.

SOMETHING IN THE FOREST

This forest is stiff with immigrants' memories.
The Irish, Italians, Chinese, Scandinavians.
They remember the smells of sweat, the sounds
        of saws biting, of swaths lined
Through the stability of preexistent peace.
           They witnessed rails set down on bald ground,
           rails gleaming with purpose, clanged
Into change by hammers swung with songs learned
        in old country youth and sung in languages
        beginning to be forgotten.

Let us escape, you and I, at least for now,
Make camp in a secret valley on a crisp stream
        where love crackles on the face
        of a time-honored fire, its flames
Twisting up into a pilgrim sky that flows with twilight pastels
Pulled westward over the tree-ridged horizon
        by a guileless and faithful sun.

MAKAH COUNTRY

I live in Makah country, my brothers, the wind and sea.
The mussel shell carries our song
Across to the April seal migrating north,
Its fur, its meat, dark and lean.

The seal waits upon my prayer
To the Creator of Daylight, the One,
Who will decide if we are worthy of the seal
So that he will give himself to us.

Above us the tall forests of the Olympic
Hurl down wild plants, medicines, and evergreens
Filled with huckleberry, salal berry,
But mostly the great cedar upon which we depend.

My sister Keena walks the summer beach.
The low tide permits periwinkle, limpets, barnacles,
And sea urchin; she smiles, her basket filled,
Her harvest from the past, present, and future.

When the fish call, my brothers and I
Take our hooks of steam-bent wood
And cherry bark to pull sweet rock cod,
Halibut, the coho, steelhead, and blueback.

We trust in Thunderhead, who beats
His wings into thunder, his eyes into lightning.
When we need his help and that of the One,
He will carry a whale in his talons to our beach.

MIDDLEBURY JULY

The only storm you can hear today
is from the deck of the Storm Café,
the one roaring from the flashy-faced water
as it dances out of control before leaping over the falls
into the void, into the arms of gravity.

You sit with tourists and summer language
students consuming exotic sandwiches,
eloquent soups, and racy salads.
Young waitresses flit from table to table,
Boys skip flat stones off Otter Creek,
And on the Marble Works footbridge,
strollers point to the free-falling water
suspended for only miniscule fractions
of time, its mass crashing below,
all foamed-up from the experience.

Pieces of this gray-bearded town pull you in:
New England churches, the phlegmatic
stores ensconced on Main Street, the dairy cows,
sheep, and Morgan horses all working the rich soil
of the Champlain Valley; Middlebury College
birthed back in 1800 by young Congregational ministers
from Yale, the tough, contemptuous Adirondacks
peering this way from the west and the softer Green Mountains
hinting you may have, at last, arrived in Shangri-la.

It's the peace, yes, that's what it is,

the peace you crave after fighting in some
other life or in the jungles of a frenzied
city you have decided you must flee.
You will be able to haul yourself out of your limitations,
bathe your wounds in resonant streams, float down
moist trails carpeted with scented pine needles
and hug resolute boulders, touch pubescent moss,
get to know chatty chipmunks, sassy ferns,
and venerable hardwoods—all seemingly
fashioned from God's pure, cool breath.

SAUDI ARABIA

The wind-blown dune wanders errantly,
A wave crossing the seemingly impotent desert.
I drop on my knees and scoop umbered sand.
It slides through my fingers like cooled water.
I wash my hands in the silence of antiquity.

The grains whisper to us about tales of men
Who lifted their eyes into the haze,
Into the dust to gaze at distant horizons
Where light and time offered secrets
To those who did not fear silence,
Who could become one with themselves,
Their meditations to race across the night sky
Against the Milky Way, sail on shooting stars
Past Jupiter and Venus and Mars, their thoughts
Converted into dreams and fantasies
Created by their struggles and memories.

This sun has roasted the soil and turned it into sand.
Moisture is rejected by the hot,
Dry air, unable to form into clouds.
Men who choose to travel or live on these barrens
Must follow the commandments of the sun.
They recognize how the ancients would
Assemble and worship Shamash, hoping
He would present game and wild grain
And point to those watered places where
The living would be able to endure.

The Bedouins, their bravery proportioned
To survival, ready to revenge insults and injuries,
Offer cardamom tea in small ceramic cups,
Tender lamb cooked slowly on rocks, bread baked
In the sand so loose it falls away when patted.
The herd of camels brays in their own language,
Talk to relatives, discussing the day's events.
North and east, oil, the thick black waters
Spread underneath, is converted into riyals
And gives Riyadh its trappings of civilization.
Fresh water, cleansed of salt, greens
The city, its avenues, parks, and people.

Saudi men are clothed in white thobes,
Their heads covered with red-flecked goutras.
What women we see are gowned in black,
Only faces or eyes to be viewed by others.
The day is spaced by prayers, the men
Prostrate themselves five times to Allah.
The souks are composed of shops,
Filled with merchants, traders, and artisans.

This kingdom is no longer an abstraction,
Its people not mysterious, only different,
As we are to them and to other peoples.
There are princes here who deal in friendship;
Who share, like with family, like with family.

SITKA

From Asia, Baranov and his wild-eyed
Russians struck the Tlingits and Haidas,
Emasculated and homogenized these tribes,
Forcing on them the Russian Orthodox Church
And its culture, conquerors converting the infidels.
Now these Alaskans sell wooden dolls and trinkets
To camera-carrying explorers off cruise ships.

Sitka snuggles down in front of mountains
That flatten out into a harbor protected by spunky
Spruce-laden islands prepared for defense.
High up, fields of snow made from the whitest
Of whites hide unforgiving crevices.
Sharp-angled granite breaks the skyline.
Jagged peaks and chines dare climbers.

The salmon never listened to anyone, slipping
By men and bears, bent on reproductive missions.
Sea otters, lionized seals, and whales ply the waters,
Their careers narrowed and specialized by time.

Black ravens trade trails with bold bald eagles
And dash across a scrubbed sky, these titans
Floating on air fat with clarity and purpose.
Quiescence pervades, hanging over everything.
Time itself becomes timeless.

ON THE ALPINE HIGHLANDS

The wind lies naked against the Engelmann spruce
And Douglas pine, sucking out moisture and ambition.
Soon it sprints away, off to check out
Smiling wildflowers and boulders
Breeding on the alpine meadows.

I sit, an unregistered guest in the white
Blackout of mountain-topped clouds,
Sight elk standing proudly, their eloquent
Racks looking like Olympic laurels.

Soon the vessel of sky wraps me inside
Its nondimensional mysteries, slowly unfolds
Its canons of behavior, discarding isolation
Together with the clamor and demands of tomorrow,
Offering instead an opportunity for silence and serenity.

TAOS REVISITED

for Jamie Bauer

This all-seeing mesa, sagebrushed in July green,
Sweeps across the almost endless plains
Under grayed rains that march in step, like buffalo
So thick the ground is no longer fully visible.

The sky demands continual attention and obeisance,
Planning what happens next, its creativity and skills
A solid reminder where ultimate control resides.
Talk about ego and I'll give you the sky every time.

To ensure its dominance the heavens dispatch electric bolts.
Bellowing thunder follows as if lightning is not enough.
The feelings it creates are strange and mysterious.
Things occur today as if great meaning is attached.

The Taos Pueblo Indians knew the evergreened
Sangre De Cristo Mountains were where the gods live.
Georgia O'Keeffe understood the magnificent thunderstorms,
The skulls of cattle, their horns and hollowed-out eyes.

THE LONER

Naples, 1949

In those early mornings, cooled by night's
saturating sleep, before the rivers
of air spill summer's heavy-eyed heat,
before his legs become weighted down,
before his arms tire from carrying the post-*fascisti*
blocks up ladders to masons yelling down,
Giuseppe thinks of Saturday afternoons
dressed in his one suit, thickened
in year-round wool, his face scrubbed
from the week's contemptible humiliations,
his black hair washed and slicked down,
the gray shadows of dust and dreariness
discarded like wandering ghosts who finally
reject their unenviable tasks,
Giuseppe Fillanti, the one who rarely speaks,
this noble knight emerges to strut
like Nero and Marcus Aurelius and Patton,
and march down a *decumati* in the old town
past a sacred temple where priests
shuddered under crumbling roofs
smoldering with deities no longer fashionable.

Where does he travel, his quick, firm steps
so different from those of other *napoletani*
who shed ambition and cling to floors
that have escaped the afternoon's scorch?

Giuseppe Fillanti journeys in triumph to the opera,
there to ascend the penultimate heights
that float between nothing and infinity,
there to lie with friendly and impassioned gods,
together to feast and play and love.

SCENE

Summer sun splashes on this delusory
Seurat-sea bouncing off frothed
Fronts of cresting waves
Their tight claws pouncing on the brazen beach.
Through bottoms of hairy eyebrows
Squinting eyes observe ripened shore grass
Swaying in unexplained patterns to muted music
Orchestrated by puffs of gusts pushed out
Of the east and arranged by that same
Source that sponsored this morning.

A flag unfurls held stiff by the wind.
On a flagpole it pierces the horizon
Where the sky begins while a mockingbird mimics
Everyone's songs and that analyzer in my brain
Is punching out so many cards
I cannot read them all so fast.

THE LONGHOUSE

Post and lintel structure
in perfect mathematical balance,
Twelve foot by twenty-four,
Its simplicity thousands of years old.

This Scandinavian longhouse,
Stolid posts, hearty beams
Joining with rafters framed into
Triangles that support the gabled roof,

Angles down from the peak past
Stalwart walls to end gracefully in soffits.
Classic, basic shelter conceived
So far back we hardly know when.

I write my poems here, away from people
And phones and computers and time,
Content, happy, my ears sharpened
With wind sounds and bird calls.

I am alone but not lonely,
Rather returned to simpler times,
With ancestors who might speak
To me now that I can hear them.

IV

THE WAY FORWARD,
THE WAY BACK

MATHEMATICS FOR A RAINY MORNING

Thick rain penetrates the stuffed air
        and scrubs it clean.
Every drop has agreed to begin
        with two hydrogen, one oxygen atom
        in perfect combination,
Free-falling, thirty-two feet per second/second.
They crash onto the deck, vanishing
        like spent cells,
Their eloquent lives consumed in just small minutes.

Look: on the pond, drops bang the surface,
Their craters expanding into circles that flatten out
        as if what happened hadn't.
Others will repeat this behavior, ordained robots
Balancing equations of moisture and temperature,
Fulfilling their responsibility to the constancy
        of mathematics.

WINTER'S ELOQUENCE

Winter is impeccably white and elegant.
Its pronouncement offered today is
         snow,
            cold sandy granules
Fashioned from a disheveled sky.

Farmhouse smoke rises like a twisting serpent,
Sliding up slowly into eternity.
             The clever wind,
              that persistent artist,
Sculpts miniature ridges and valleys
That undulate across the meadow.

ON A CLEAR WINTER NIGHT

I

the snow broods quietly
then catches sight
of a deer
peering out
then emerging slowly.

II

the year's apples
red and white
like red and white stars
washing
pressed light
back into
the ubiquitous snow.

FOUR FOR WINTER

I

Black crow
Crosses grayed sky.
Whitened fields are edged
With even-tempered trees.

II

Snow sniffs and filters the air.
Its tiny feathers
Transform what it embraces
Into the purest white of whites.

III

Winds sit patiently
In the northwest
Scheming when
To thrash the land.

IV

Winter releases its power.
Most things seek silence.
Coyotes call out their night voices
Invading our spirits.

MUSIC OF THE MEADOW

Come with me. We'll wrap ourselves
        inside this meadow,
Hiding from the wind's breath
That like rain, moves and changes
        what it touches.
Like with leaves that sway to ancient rhythms.

Over there, somewhere out of sight,
        an August robin quietly teaches
Her children about inherited two-note songs.
In their minuscule homes crickets congregate,
Arguing like disgruntled relatives.
Carefully concealed in the pond, overstuffed
        frogs bawl nonsense
        only they seem to understand.

JANUARY TWILIGHT

Something about the way
Light spills out
Of this unruffled day
A little like the way
A plump life fades out
After a grandiose good-bye.
Tomorrow becomes another today.
Other lives will enter.
Maybe one will be mine.
Or one will be yours.

I need to catch my breath.
Serenity softens time's indifference.
Light colors the bay and sculptured boulders
Grow larger, granted permission
By the autocratic tide.
Canada geese, scaup, and gulls lounge
Half-sleeping in their saltwater chairs.
Everything pretends to be timeless.
I wish you could be here with me.

GREAT WHITE PINE

Your wisdom is held
In your fat-skinned trunk
In your opened arms.
Teach me, staunch friend.
Be with me forever.

THE FOG

I face the edge of a void,
No seam between earth and sky.
Behind me ancient sunstorms echo.

A pause in eternity, then

A little duck launches alone
Accelerates low over the water,
Climbs quickly from the past,
His purpose penetrating the gray.

Small being,
I wish you joy, safe journey.
Give me courage for my own.

I watch
As my love pushes through
The fog and breaks
Pure and clean into the sky

Now shouldered with thick-bodied
Clouds black and ominous.
The duck continues unafraid

Until a double rainbow holds it,
Each carrying the colors of life
While behind lightning breaks the serenity.

STEARMAN

A man's name has become a plane,
A biplane, perfectly formed,
Sitting up on stiff front legs,
A little like a sassy colt.
You prime four strokes into
The impatient engine,
Listen for its cough, then the roar
As your plane greets you once more.
You're convinced it smiles only at you.

On the runway you ask for speed.
She begins her roll; soon you lift
The tail as she flexes
Her arms and rises off the earth
Into a sort of eternity
Where you've always wanted to be.
And now you are.

You sail on yellow Navy wings
Over fields sporting greens and browns.
Together you hang in space, balanced
By gravity and your engine's steady power.
You float naked and pristine
On mysterious winds you can never
See but have learned to understand.

You have feelings you cannot really
Share, but back down on the ground
You and the other biplane pilots
Grin that very special grin.

AT FIVE HUNDRED FEET,
NEW YORK TO FLORIDA

I fly my Boeing Stearman WW II biplane,
Caress the warmth, waft, and sashay
Through the moist, fattened air
Like a youngster surfing on friendly waves.

The wind is contributed by Heaven,
Breathes against my face, my helmet and goggles.
The engine declares its power, stunning the air.
Its pitch is irrevocable and reassuring.

At five hundred feet, I slide over
Grain and tobacco fields that pray
To summer and yearn for the rays
To impregnate the eager ground.

My mind roves over territories owned
By eloquent oaks and esteemed evergreens,
Huddled and whispering parents
Devoted to their children's futures.

I wing past barrier islands entrenched
Off the Carolinas, Georgia, and Florida,
Some still pristine unpeopled habitats
For porpoises, birds, deer, and wild horses.

WINGS

Life is lifted
into my wings
its energy wafts
through my body

                I surf on the wind
                my wondrous playmates
                clouds shaped by imagination
                here
                time is at peace

WINTER STORM

faintly in the dimmed distance
like in a dream when you're not sure
if you heard or saw something
the striking sounds of canada geese
fight the wind and the snow flies
sideways deciding to challenge
gravity

the sky and land merge into one
indistinguishable except for the purity
of white the snow spreads over the ground
even the bay gets involved and pretends
the sky is an illusion that cannot
last

you cannot quite tell which direction
the geese are flying but remember
they form a V you cannot tell
which ones will find the grass they need
to survive the winter you cannot tell
which ones will die and pay the price
for not migrating but you do know
nature is unmoved intractable
and always invokes the lessons of
reality

WINTERSCAPE

The year's final
   project
fashions featherlike
   flakes
out of today's ruffled
   sky.

Farmhouse smoke rises
   like an affable serpent
in some Arthurian myth
   twisting and turning
toward one of the eternities.
   The clever wind
that practiced and persistent artist
   sculpts snow
into miniature mountains
   their tiny ridges
sweeping down into diminutive valleys
   that undulate
across the field in delicate waves
   whispering
to things that wait
   patiently underneath
ready to burst open bold and sassy
   when spring takes its turn.

THE WAY FORWARD, THE WAY BACK

The leaf hesitates then pitches forward
From the ash tree onto my deck and acts confused
Not sure of its way down.
The way it's supposed to go used up
Bleeding away its rusted roan the green
Of past youth forgotten those carefree
Radiant rash days when age didn't matter.
Someone called me I think I was shaving.
I can't even remember who it was.
Something about money something about
How I should send a check how important it was.
I wanted to send busted glass instead.
Colored glass from the beach polished with reality.
There are old and new things to learn.
Like in that epic poem about Gilgamesh and Enkidu.
Would they take on the gods today?
Were they lovers or just inseparable friends?
Shakespeare should have written a play
About their tragedy of ancient Uruk.
I'd like to smell them in battle but my nose is starved.
Max my dog could; he'd understand but wouldn't tell.
All right I'll leave now with my brand of dissension.
Maybe join up with that law-abiding leaf
No less confused and try to find my own way
Down to that incorruptible beach

Where driftwood chronicles disordered lives
Where shells remember former housekeepers
Where salt swims and tastes time before moving
Out into the universe on its mission to deliver the leaf.

ABOUT THE AUTHOR

Donald Everett Axinn was born in New York City. He grew up on Long Island and spent some early years near Fort Huachuca in Arizona. After graduating from Middlebury College, he served as a strategic intelligence officer in the U.S. Army Reserve Corps, and later as a university dean. He is the recipient of four honorary doctorates from Middlebury, Hofstra, Southern Vermont College and the State University of New York.

A film is in process for *Spin*, and a screenplay for a third novel, *Allan, Burning*. Axinn's poems and articles have appeared in literary journals and newspapers, including the *New York Times* and *Newsday*. He was awarded the Tennessee Williams Fellowship in Poetry from the Bread Loaf Writers' Conference. He has served on numerous boards, including Farrar, Straus & Giroux, Poets & Writers, The Poetry Society of America, The American Academy of Poets, Hofstra University, and the Cradle of Aviation Museum, and chaired the Long Island chapter of The Nature Conservancy. He is an avid pilot, who flies a 1932 Waco UBA biplane, a Super Cub, and a classic World War II Stearman biplane.

Mr. Axinn lives on Long Island and in Florida and Vermont.